CASH FOR GOLD

HOW TO SET UP

AS

A GOLD TRADER

David Barnato

Copyright David Rawson-Wheater October 2013
dwheater@lantic.net

THE GOLDEN RULES ABOUT BUYING AND SELLING GOLD

MAKE $1000 A WEEK PART TIME

Full time you could become a millionaire.

ALL THE SECRET FACTS FROM 'MR GOLD.'

'CASH 4 GOLD': HOW TO GET INTO THE BUSINESS.

- HOW TO MAKE MONEY EVEN IF THE MARKET FALLS
- HOW TO VALUE GOLD.
- HOW TO FIND SELLERS.
- HOW TO FIND BUYERS.
- PART TIME OR FULL TIME.
- ANY AGE.
- TRADE FROM HOME OR SMALL SHOP.
- HOW TO TEST DIAMONDS.
- HOW TO BE AN ETHICAL PAWN BROKER.
- TRADE FROM ANYWHERE IN THE WORLD

MARKETING

Gold is the ultimate precious metal that is recognized anywhere in the world. It's value may rise or fall in the short term, but long term it has steadily risen. In the troubled times that we now live in a hidden holding in gold is essential. It doesn't rust or rot and because of gold's high value per ounce, it doesn't take up much space. When the bubble in stock markets comes to an end as it surely will, the value of gold will soar because when paper assets fall, investors turn to gold.

However, one of the great things about setting up as a gold trader is that you can still make money if the gold price falls, although with skill and luck you will make a lot more when markets rise.The reason is that you are buying low and selling high and very quickly. Thus buying and selling gold is a very low risk business and you can set up for as little as $1000. Incidentaly I have written this guide using dollars in respect of costs, returns etc, but the principles remain the same wherever you are in the world. You can be a young person starting a first business or a retired person struggling to stretch your pension. You can be male or female many Gold Traders are women. You must of course be careful about security and use commom sense. If you follow this guide you will make a handsome living or even get very rich. However, for legal reasons I cannot guarantee your success, that will be down to you, but many others have succeeded using these principles.The facts and figures quoted cannot be guaranteed, but every endeavor has been made to be accurate. What is certain is that this business really works!

To start you will need the following items:

1 A set ofsmall jewelers' scales

2 An acid testing set

3 Magnifying glass. This can be a jeweler's eye glass or an illuminated large magnifying glass.

4. Diamond Tester

5. file

6. a magnet

Total cost should be well under $500

You will also need a receipt book and a separate book to keep a record of what you have bought. This is not only for your own records, but in most countries you will be obliged to keep one anyway. Don't be tempted to leave some entries out to hide trades from the tax man. Not only is the tax environment getting tougher everywhere, but as you expand and hold more stock you will probably be able to rollover extra stock and delay tax. You must take professional advice, but in my opinion you only need to worry about tax if you aren't making enough profit to owe any!

Of course you will need some trading capital to buy your gold with. The more the better, but in the early days you can sell your purchases quickly and buy more stock with the original capital and the profit. You could start with as little as $500,and after about twelve trades you should now have $5000 which is a perfect amount to trade with.

The first thing to realize is that there are two gold prices. There is the bullion price, also known as 'spot' gold and there is the scrap price which is the price at which you will buy. On average the scrap price is 45% of the bullion price, thus it is a good profit margin business.

So, why is there such a gap between the 'spot' price of gold and the scrap price? First one must consider quantity. Bullion is sold in solid pure gold bars that require a considerable investment. Scrap gold can be a ring with only 30% pure gold and weighing as little as one gram. Incidentally, the term scrap does not mean necessarily damaged items. Any second hand jewelry is valued as scrap, unless there are precious stones involved and even if a diamond ring of good value cost $100'000 when bought from a jewelers shop, it's value if sold back into the trade could be as little as $20'000. The difference between the retail and 'wholesale' price of a piece of jewelry is enormous. This particularly applies to an item bought new and then sold second hand, but even a second hand piece will fetch much less than you paid for it, unless you bought it as a dealer at the trade price.

As a Cash For Gold Trader you will exclude the value of the stones in jewelry items and either deduct the stones estimated weight from the total gold price, unless you are considering a high quality item such as for example a diamond necklace. Until you become experienced you should ask the customer if you can get a second opinion if you are offered an obvious high value item; ' As you want to give the best price'. If you are presentable and look honest most people will agree to this However, those with cheaper items will usually be looking for fast deals. So you need to find a jeweler who will advise you about high value items and hopefully buy from you. This will not be as difficult as you might imagine as many jewelers make a lot of money buying and selling quality items.However, in the beginning of your business you will mainly get rings with 'costume' stones. You dont want to buy these stones as they have little value. However, it is common to buy the ring as it is and deduct something from the overall weight. You make an offer based on that. In other words you want the stones for nothing or the customer can keep them.

Diamonds are easy to deal with as a diamond tester costs very little and when the point is touched on the diamond it will either be silent or 'ping' if the stone really is a diamond.Some tsters have two completely diferent sounds for each possibility. Incidentally you need to be very careful that you only touch the stone with the tester. If you touch the mounting you will get a false reading and think that you are buying a diamond.Also, you must not touch the diamond with the tester point at an angle or you may get a false reading. The tester must be held so that the end is pointing downwards and you touch the middle of the diamond. Full instructions come with a diamond tester so don't worry about it at this stage.Suppliers of jewelers' accessories can be found easily on the internet and you can either collect or get what you need posted.

Care is needed in taking out the stones that you intend to keep. A small file is the best thing to use.Gently push back whatever is holding the ring and carefully prise the stone out.At first this will seem rather daunting, but if it is a ring that you are selling on as scrap with a stone of little value it doesn't matter if you botch it up. Real diamonds are very hard so there is little chance of damaging them so don't regard this as a huge obstacle.

Most diamonds in rings are very small and worth surprisingly little. A typical tiny diamond is worth about $5. A very small diamond is worth about $10. Larger diamonds can of course be worth very much more depending on the quality which we will discuss further on.

Most of the gold that you buy will be sold to a refining company who will pay you about 95% of the pure gold price. You will remove the stones and keep them in a safe place and perhaps sell them once a year just before Christmas. However, as this is what most gold traders do it might be better to chose another time of year to collect your bonus. Sometimes the seller will want to keep the stone. The amount that you will pay the customer is based on the weight of the gold and thus when the price is without the stone you will need to make an offer based on an estimation of the stones weight and deduct that weight from your total figure. However, most stones weigh very little so this is not too critical. Personally, I weigh the item and make an offer based on the total weight. In other words I am paying the gold weight for the stone and this will be very little.

Incidentally, the most valuable stones are diamonds, then emeralds and rubies. All of these stones can be man made and look like the real thing. Be very wary of dealing in stones without a trustworthy second opinion. If however you are buying an item with stones and you can't get a second opinion, just pay the current gold price depending on the weight and quality of the gold. The quality of gold refers to the density or karats. This is the term used for the amount of pure gold in an item. You will almost never be offered pure gold which contains just under 24 karats of gold. An item which is 9ct gold will rarely have a valuable stone.

The reason for the different karats is that by adding metals to the gold mix the cost of the item to manufacture is reduced the less gold is added. The reason is of course about marketing as most people cannot tell by looking how many karats of gold there are in a given item. Jewelers usually know the karat of an item by slight color variations caused by the amount of non gold used. This is very subtle and sometimes even jewelers can be wrong. Even the stamp inside the ring or on one of the clasps on a bracelet or necklace doesn't prove that the item is solid gold of a specific number of karats. Crooks abound who can add a stamp saying 9ct or 375 which is the number that relates to 9ct solid gold. Also, even 'reputable' dealers sometimes add the stamp for 9ct or the words nine karat with the letter 'plated' added. Also, it is possible to remove the word 'plated' leaving 9ct or 18ct etc. So beware!

HOW TO TEST GOLD FOR KARAT VALUE

To test the purity of a gold item there are several ways. The best is a very expensive electronic tester which will set you back about $50000. The less expensive way is to buy a small gold testing kit from a jewelers' supplier. For about $100. This will consist of a battery operated gold tester and two bottles of acid. There is a small indentation on the tester and you add one drop of activator and three drops of the other acid supplied. When you switch the machine on a message will read 'not gold'. This is because you havn't yet tested anything. Attach the crocodile clips to the item to be tested. You then dip a portion of the item in the mixed acid If the item is not solid gold the appropriate message will remain, reading 'not gold.'. If it is solid gold the machine will show the karat weight. To be certain of a correct reading always clean the item with a jewelers cloth and rub on the jewelers 'block which comes with the gold kit or make a very small mark with a file. This to enable the acid to read what is beneath the surface. If you are careful you will be able to polish the mark out of the item if the customer doesn't want to sell. Be very careful about handling acid, it only stings a little and scrubs off in about three days, but I am sure that it isn't good for the skin!

The third alternative and the cheapest is to buy a very cheap kit that contains several bottles of acid, one for each karat weight. Inside you will also find a small black plate and after cleaning the item to be tested you rub it on the plate and then add a drop of each of the acids. The one that remains clear is the karat weight of the item.

An even cheaper alternative is just to buy a bottle of acid gold tester and to put a drop on the item. If it is not solid gold the acid will turn green.

However, as with most things in life nothing is perfect and it is possible that an item such as a watch may read as solid gold on the electronic tester but in fact be gold plated. Perhaps thick gold plate, but unless it is a Rolex or one of the other classic watches it will have little value.

To avoid buying gold plate you should take a small file and discretely file into the gold as discussed above. On a ring you obviously make the mark on the inside where it will not be visible. Necklaces and bracelets are more tricky and you must make a test on two places. If the acid test shows that it is solid gold then it probably is, but if in doubt because of the light weight or color or even the look of the customer just don't buy it! Be especially careful about gold necklaces as these are difficult to test. Also, watches can be deceiving. Rings are usualy straightforward and the acid test is sufficient to show that it is solid gold or not.

THE FIRST GOLDEN RULE: IF IN DOUBT DON'T BUY IT!

As a guide most rings offered will be gold, but some won't be. The very first simple test with rings is to test with a magnet.

THE SECOND GOLDEN RULE: IF IT STICKS TO THE MAGNET IT'S NOT SOLID GOLD!

With necklaces you have to test in at least two places and beware that sometimes the hook and eye may be solid gold but the chain isn't.

Watches are usually gold plate. Look up the make on the internet whilst the customer waits. You will always find some second hand prices for most makes. If the prices are low don't buy it. If the name is known like Rolex then it will still be worth a good price. Internet prices will give you an indication. Remember that the price new of good quality watches will be many times their second hand value. For example a new Gents

Rolex perpetual oyster, part gold and part steel is about $15000. Second hand you will buy one for about $3000. In the trade you will buy one for under $2000.If you are taking one in pawn you would lend about $1000

There are many other watches some of which are worth more than Rolex. Most people have never heard of them, but here are a few. Use the internet to find values. Breilting; Omega; Baume et Mercier; Frederique Constant; Breguet Jaeger-LeCoutre;Thomas Tampion; Raymond Weil; Waltham Watch Conpany and many others.

THIRD GOLDEN RULE: BE ON THE LOOKOUT FOR FAKE WATCHES.

YOU CAN OFTEN TELL A FAKE BECAUSE THE FINISH ISN'T QUITE RIGHT, IT MIGHT BE VERY SLIGHTLY ROUGH IN PLACES WHEN YOU RUN YOUR FINGERS OVER THE SURFACE AND JOINS. ALSO, GOLD SMELLS SLIGHTLY DIFERENT FROM GOLD PLATE, BUT IT WILL TAKE YOU A LONG TIME TO LEARN THIS ART. BUT IF YOU ARE CONSIDERING A BIG BUDGET ITEM GET A SECOND SKILLED OPINION BEFORE BUYING. IF IN DOUBT DON'T BUY!

To learn more about rare watches and their values go on to Amazon. There are a number of good books available. There are also books on the value of old jewelry. Schroeder Publishing is one.

We must now talk in more detail about the various karats of gold. This is of course important as the percentage of pure gold in the ring or whatever is critical to the value. The following are the percentages of pure gold in the various karat categories.

First a short note about what 'karat' means. Oddly enough it comes from the words carob seed which was originally used to balance the scales in oriental bazars.

So karats mean the percentage of gold in an item. The value of pure gold as bullion is based in US dollars per ounce. However as a Gold Trader you will buy and sell in grams. There are 28.350 grams in an ounce of gold. On the internet you will easily find charts which show the given number of grams per ounce and the values in several currencies. You will of course need to check the gram prices every day at least once. Gold bullion has been known to move hundreds of dollars in a matter of moments. This is however very unusual, most moves will be relatively small and you will only be marginally affected if prices fall before you sell on.

PERCENTAGES OF PURE GOLD FOR VARIOUS KARATS AND THE NUMERICAL MARKS

8 ct 333	33.3% pure gold	The gold mark
9 ct 375	37.5% pure gold.	The gold mark is
10 ct 416	41.67% pure gold	The gold mark is
12 ct 500	50% pure gold	The gold mark is
14 ct 583	58.33% pure gold	The gold mark is
18 ct 750	75% pure gold	The gold mark is
22 ct 916	91.67% pure gold	The gold mark is
24 ct 999	99% pure gold	The gold mark is

HOW GOLD IS VALUED

Obviously the price of gold is based on supply and demand. In this global world of instant information the price of gold bullion will rise on rumors of war and sometimes fall if lots of money is going into stock markets. Generally however most investors will hold a long term position with a portion of their wealth in gold just in case there is a world economic crisis and paper money is no longer trusted. In recent years the amount of physical gold being hoarded in China and India has risen steadily. At the moment this buying of physical gold is a small portion of all the gold traded. Most gold is now on paper. In theory gold depositories who issue certificates of deposit showing that the holder has X ounces of gold stored should have a matching amount of gold. The depository makes an annual charge for holding and insuring the gold. However, rumors have circulated recently that not all gold vaults have the amount of gold that all their certificates show. One report claimed that if all the gold held on paper was added up it would be 40 times more than all the gold ever mined.

If true, these rumors are very disturbing and possibly a grave danger to the world economy. What is even more disturbing is that many bank experts claim that even if true it would be quite legal! They point out that licensed banks are allowed by law to lend many times the amount of cash and assets that they hold. Thus if the XXXX bank holds $100 million in cash , depending on the rules of the country in which it is based it could lend as much as $1000million. So how does it do this in practice? It prints money. Thus if it is possible to print money against assets that do not match the assets actually owned by the bank it is probably legal to issue gold certificates against gold that the bank doesn't hold. The banks deny all of this, but if true and suddenly it became generally believed and there was a 'run' on the bank to get the gold back that clients owned there would be a huge crisis.

One consequence would probably be that physical gold would soar in value as the value of paper gold evaporated. However it would be quite difficult to swop a gold bar for a month's rent or a basket of groceries. This is perhaps why Kruger rand have become such a popular way to own gold. Each Kruger is one ounce of pure gold and trades at a modest premium. If times get tough it would be very useful to have a lot of ordinary gold rings to trade with. So when you go into this business make a plan to hold a portion back for a rainy day. However, you must take the long term view. Although gold has always risen with inflation there are periods when prices fall for years, so you need to be very emotionally strong to stick to this plan.

So the value of gold is determined by international demand and priced in US dollars. However at street level the buying and selling of small quantities of gold is done in grams and often in the local currency. For a gold trader to calculate his buying in price you only need to consult the internet. There you will find the price per ounce and in grams. The price will be in dollars and a simple chart shows you the value converted into several currencies.

The value shown is of course the spot price for pure gold. Thus if you are making an offer on a 9ct gold item which contains only 37.5% of gold you will calculate what this means in terms of the retail value, how much the smelter will pay and work out the difference which is your profit and how much you will offer the customer.

EG. Gold ring weighs 5 grams. The price of pure spot gold today is $1400 an ounce. This works out at about $493 per gram. So the ring would be worth $2469 if it were pure gold. The smelter will pay you 95% of this which comes to $2345. After checking very carefully that it really was 24 karats you would offer 45% of the value which would be $1055 your profit would thus be $1290.

EG Gold ring weighs 5 grams. The price of pure spot gold today is $1400 an ounce. However, your acid test shows that it is 9ct. Thus the ring only contains 37.5% of pure gold. Doing the calculation manually you will see that 37.5% of the per ounce price is $525 and this comes to $185 per gram. The total retail value of the ring is therefore $925. Thus you would offer $416. Your profit would be $509.

The above examples show what a substantial profit can be made in a normal market. However, if you have a lot of competition you would increase the price based on percentage to perhaps 50% of the retail value. Even 55% to the client leaves a good margin.

EG. Gold weighs 5 grams. The price of pure spot gold today is $1400 an ounce or $185 per gram. The ring is 9ct retail value is therefore $925. You pay 55% which is $509. Your profit would be $416. Still pretty good.

The term 'spot' gold means gold tradeable immediately for cash. A great deal of gold is bought or sold for future sale or acquisition. Some of these 'future options' are bought as insurance. For example if you hold a lot of gold but you feel that there may be a fall over the next few months you can sell an option to buy. If gold falls then you keep the option money. If the price rises you have to sell at the agreed price which will obviously be advantageous to the option buyer. However, you keep the option premium. The technical term for an option to sell is a 'put' and an option to buy is called a 'call'. Although options are gambles, they can be useful under certain circumstances as insurance

HOW TO GET STARTED AS A CASH FOR GOLD TRADER

Gold dealing is a good business to be in. You buy gold at 'scrap' price which is about 45% of the bullion price. You sell it to the refiners, who will usually pay about 95% of the final absolutely pure weight. Thus your gross profit after you have paid 45% to the seller and 5% to the refiner is about 50%.

Even if the price of gold goes down you are unlikely to lose anything because of the high margin. If the price of gold goes up whilst you are holding it then you can make a lot of money. In many ways it's the perfect business. You can start by just running small classified ads and trade from home with few overheads. Alternatively you can rent a small shop at low rent because you need little space. Or you may well be able to rent space in another larger shop, such as dry cleaners, furniture etc. If the shop owner is particularly helpful he may build you a small cubicle. This can be very small, as little as 9 foot by 9. [Roughly three meters by three meters] Whichever route you go overheads should be low.

Gold dealing is not a difficult business to learn, just follow the instructions in this guide and you may well become a millionaire. However, like all businesses there are risks, but they can be minimized. The worst risk is that you may buy an item thinking that it is solid gold and then it turns out to be plate. Follow my instructions of checking and this will never happen. However, when I first started the risk wasn't explained fully enough to me and on my first day of being left on my own a chap came in with a lump of gold the size of a golf ball. It looked like lots of small bits of gold that had been fused together to make one piece. I checked with the acid and it didn't go green but I was a bit nervous about it and so I hesitated about offering a price because it was a substantial weight. To overcome my reluctance the seller made a very, very low price proposition. It was irresistible and so a deal was done. Had I done the correct thing and used a file to get beneath the surface the truth would have soon been revealed as it was of course 'fools gold' which shines like gold but is worthless. The seller had cleverly plated the lump and today it stands on my desk as a paper weight. A very expensive paper weight, but much more importantly a very good lesson.

As a Gold Trader you are not limited to buying rings and of course you may buy silver items. However gold is generally more lucrative and you will buy chains, bracelets odd cuff links or odd ear rings, old watches and broken items.

If you decide to start from home, using the telephone and small adds your overheads will be very low. However, don't have buyers calling. There is a security risk. You could meet in Starbucks, McDonalds, or even better somewhere that has seating with some privacy. Be very discrete and don't let others see the jewelry that you are considering. Fortunately the small electronic scales, tester and acids come in small boxes.

The first thing is to test with a magnet and look for a gold mark such as 375. If the item passes the test then weigh it and make an offer subject to testing with acid. If the client accepts do the test and quietly swap the cash for the gold.

If you decide to start trading in this way your ads should be short and catchy. When I started like this I advertised a very good 18ct price. In theory this should be double the 9ct price but by making it more than double it is eye catching to those people who have seen others' gold prices, which will usually be double. My thinking is that although your percentage of profit on the 18ct price will be a lower percentage, the actual cash profit is about the same. For example if the spot price for 9ct gold is $155 a gram, you will offer perhaps $100 .Giving you a profit of $55 The spot price for 18ct will be therefore $310 per gram. If you offer $250 a gram for 18ct you will make a profit of $60. A smaller margin, but a slightly higher profit and good way to attract sellers.

Although working from home is a good way to start it is certainly not the most productive. People like to go to shops that they have seen when passing by. However, it is a gentle way to get into the business and if you decide to do so your first small advertisement could read:

GOLD WANTED

$250 per gm

+ or –

For 18ct

Call Mr. Goldman…………

When you are ready for shop premises you must decide if you are to be part or full time.

If part time you should look to rent space in a bigger shop such as furniture or a dry cleaners etc. Many shops will listen to this proposition if they think that not only will it bring in more traffic, but also a bit of rent as well. When I took this step the shop owner built me a small office 3 by 3 with a simple security gate and it worked well.

At first I started part time with a sign on my gate saying 'GOLD BUYER HERE BETWEEN 10.30 and 12.30. OR LATER BY APPOINTMENT.

This worked quite well but when I decided to be full time business increased dramatically. There is no golden rule about what hours customers will come in. Equally some days of the week can be better than others but there is no golden rule. Although towards the end of the month is slightly better than the middle, the one definite fact is that you may get very few callers in a day, but it only takes a few customers to make a handsome living. Unless you are lucky enough to have a very secure strongroom take your stock home and store it in several different places. To reduce risk many gold traders open a little later than the other local shops and close a little earlier. This reduces the risk of robbery considerably. Also, carry that day's purchases in a carrier bag amongst the shopping and in one of your pockets carry a few items of costume jewelry. These you give if you have to.

Personally I never had a security a problem. A much greater challenge was boredom. Fortunately I am a great reader so this was not such a problem for me, but think about how you are going to deal with it. In my own case I also make a point of exercising in the morning as most of the day you will be sitting down! A good brisk half hours walk sets me up for the day and weather permitting I swim when I get home.

Regarding premises a small shop of your own is the best route. Even better if you have the cash to buy it as one day you will be able to sell the business and retire on the rental from the shop.

You may think that being in a seedy area will bring in lots of desperate people. There is some truth in this, but the problem is a lot of them will be drug addicts and their items will have been stolen. Personally I have a huge moral dilemma with this. I don't like it when things are stolen from me and consequently I will never buy anything that I am suspicious about. Because of this I turn away quite a lot of business, even though my shop is not in a bad area and most customers are just temporarily down on their luck. My shop is near a supermarket and consequently it is visible and I don't need a lot of advertising spend. Wherever you set up you need traffic! Even if you are upstairs, but in a busy area provided you are allowed to put an advertising board on the pavement this will work. However, the very best route to go is to find the best small but visible shop that you can afford. Make it look respectable and comfortable and if possible make it possible for up market clients to slip in quietly and discuss their business discretely. If you have the capital invest in a neon sign . The sign could read 'GOLD WANTED'. Or 'CASH FOR GOLD.'

This brings me to the most profitable business of all. This is upmarket pawn, also known as 'buy back.' Most people in this business are greedy and unscrupulous, but it is possible to operate in an honest and ethical way and sleep at night.

The reason that this is such a good business is that if you are in the right location you will get rich customers who have lots of nice jewelry but occasionally run out of cash. Remember, you can be a multi millionaire with lots of assets, but if you run out of cash you are in trouble. This happens to more rich people than you think. And although I am not super rich it has certainly happened to me.

The normal terms for pawning is a loan about 20% lower than the 'cash for gold' price. The loan is usually for one month and a common charge is 20%. This is not per annum, but per month. Thus a diamond necklace that your friendly jeweler says is worth about $50000 in the trade will cost the customer $10000 per month. Usually pawnbrokers will extend the loan term beyond the one month, but then the cost is another $10000,-per month!

We thought a great deal about the ethics of pawning before we went into it. The good points are that it produces instant cash for the customer with no credit check, although you always need a copy of identity from every customer. Another good point for the customer is that if he can't afford to redeem the item the debt is cancelled out and he is not under the control of some loan shark with an ever rising interest debt. We still felt that the high interest charged of between 20% and 30% outrageous and so we charge 10% per month. This is still a lot of money and very profitable, but it is a useful service to most people and we are now well known for our lower 'buy back' charges.

The downside for the client is that he receives as little as 30% of the value of the item and unless he redeems and pays back both the principle and interest he has lost the item. Also, even at 10% per month it is expensive borrowing. Check your country's laws before going into this business in respect of both interest charges and the length of time that you must hold the item before selling. Sometimes it is only one month and sometimes three months .In most countries the Pawnbroker can keep the full sale price if the customer doesn't redeem. Some Pawnbrokers have a second shop which sells jewelry in a diferent area under a diferent name. The profit margin is enormous.

FOURTH GOLDEN RULE: CHECK ALL THE LEGALITIES FOR YOUR AREA

There are a number of legal points to be checked before starting both the cash for gold and pawn broking businesses. Different countries have different legal rules, but almost all will require you to obtain a 'Second Hand Dealers License' or a 'Jewelry Dealers License.' These are not usually difficult to get, but you will probably be refused if you have a criminal conviction. Incidentally, you will almost certainly need permission to put a bill board on the pavement. One small tip. Don't use boards that say 'Cash 4 Gold'. Everyone else uses them and often they also advertise using the same words. This can sometimes work against you if customers see such an advertisement and see someone else's pavement sign. Your advertising could be producing their business!

Regarding prices and profits. How much you pay per gram depends on which of the karat weights you are buying. The higher the karat the greater the percentage of gold and thus the higher the price.

Pure gold is 23.95 karats.. Jewelry is rarely pure gold because it is too soft. Jewelry is made by mixing pure gold with various other metals. The most popular mix is 9ct which means the item contains 37.5% of pure gold and the gold mark is 375. However, some genuine gold items will not have a hallmark, often because it has just worn off. Sometimes marks will be false and for example 9ct will be marked 750 to suggest that the item is 18ct.

FIFTH GOLDEN RULE: DON'T ACCEPT GOLD MARKS OR NUMBERS AT FACE VALUE.

There are unscrupulous dealers and even some manufacturers who put false stamps on items. .Check and check again with the acid test. Also, don't assume that just because there is no hallmark the item cannot be gold. Sometimes marks wear off and some foreign gold just doesn't have marks.

HOW TO SPOT GOLD PLATED WATCHES

Not all gold offered will be even 9ct-you will have to be very careful of gold plated items which have no scrap value. Watches often have a thick coat of gold plate and will give you a false reading using the electronic tester.

As mentioned earlier gold plate is easy to spot on rings by cleaning and then making a slight hidden scrape and following the procedures previously discussed.

The very first step is the magnet test, but one possible problem here is that part of the works of watches and even the back are often steel and will be picked up by the magnet. So don't rule out the possibility that the main watch and perhaps the 'inards' may be gold. Until you take off the back. If you are not experienced, taking off the back of a watch is a bit daunting and perhaps best left to your friendly jewelry mentor. If the watch is a quality one but not working, the moving parts may still have some value, but don't make an offer based on that. Carry out a test with a file so that the acid can read what's under the surface. If it's a cheap make watch [see internet for second hand prices] it is very unlikely to be solid gold. So still be wary even after the acid test.

Incidentally non famous makes of second hand watches are very difficult to sell, so have little value.

So, if you like the make of watch and it looks and feels good and you have carried out at least two gold tests then make an offer based on the weight. But until you are really experienced get a second opinion on anything for which you are offering more than $500.

SIXTH GOLDEN RULE: WEIGH THE SOLID GOLD WATCH, BUT DEDUCT 33% FOR THE NON GOLD BACK AND WORKINGS.

EVEN IF THE WATCH IS NOT WORKING THE WORKING PARTS OFTEN HAVE VALUE TO JEWELERS OR WATCHMAKERS, SO THEY WILL USUALLY HAVE VALUE, BUT DEDUCT THE 33% FROM TOTAL WEIGHT AS YOUR MAIN INTEREST IS IN BUYING GOLD AND ANYTHING EXTRA IS A USEFUL PERK.

HOW TO FIND GOLD SELLERS

Apart from customers calling in to your shop because they have seen your sign some will come because of your advertising. My experience is that lineage ads in the local people don't produce much response, but small blocks do. Leaflets given out in the area near your shop also pay for themselves and show a profit. Make sure of course that you use someone reliable to give out the leaflets. Billboards only work if they are near your shop and directional. A board outside of town on the motorway will produce almost nothing.

Television advertising is often cheaper than you would expect. This is because the most effective is late at night or in the early hours of the morning.

This is when the desperate can't sleep and usually desperation is about money or love. The possibility of selling that gold signet ring or chain shows a possible financial route. The possibility of selling the engagement ring and wedding ring given to you by a two timing husband has great emotional appeal.

Some television advertising invites people to post in their items by secure delivery and you will come back with a price. This can of course become a large scale national operation if you get it right. However, although late night TV advertising is cheap it is still a big overhead. Consequently most of the companies who operate this way pay the customer less, perhaps 30% of spot prices as opposed to your 40% or 45%. However, they seem to thrive so it must work.

The biggest risk incidentally with not only the above idea, but also building a chain of shops is staff honesty. In theory you leave your shop manager with say $5000 in the morning and pick up what he has bought at say 4pm and top up his float. There are of course ways to monitor staff but they all cost time and money. The biggest risk is the mail order idea as of course if the company never received the ring or whatever it isn't going to make an offer. However if it is recorded and just vanishes inside the office and into someones pocket or handbag there needs to be an enquiry and if too many people complain there could be serious legal issues. However, I suppose that the risk is minimized because each item is carefully listed on arrival. In the case of your own shop staff the risk is that your staff member buys the odd item or two with his own cash and then keeps the profit when he sells on. In my case each customer has to sign a receipt when he receives the cash. This can of course be disregarded by a dishonest person but it helps.

On the question of staff you should employ someone who not only has perfect references but also is well known to you or someone else that you know. Character is more important than knowledge, age, sex, or experience. I have never suffered dishonesty in this business, but I once employed a relative in another venture and she turned out to be a serious crook. Employing family is though I think a good idea if the character qualities are known to you and I do so wherever possible.

Other ways of finding gold buyers are to approach lawyers about deceased estates where there might be opportunities to make bids. Also churches are sometimes left gold in wills and also some might be persuaded to hold charity events where you would guarantee a certain price per gram.

GOLDEN RULE NUMBER 7: NEVER COMPLETELY TRUST ANYONE

TRAINING STAFF

Rule number 7 applies to customers more than staff. Almost everyone will lie if they are trying to sell something to a business person. It's human nature. Think about the lies that people say when selling cars!

Staff is another matter. Most people will 'pinch' a few paper clips, sheets of paper or pens from their employers and almost everyone steals employers' time by browsing the internet etc. This doesn't make it right, but it happens. However, most people wont steal from your stock wherever you keep it. However, there is an obligation on an employer to remove temptation wherever possible. Check stock regularly. Discuss deals done thoroughly, ask why a certain price was paid. Be in the shop as much as possible and visit regularly if you have several shops.

To teach someone the basics of this business is relatively easy. You use this guide to explain the basics of gold such as karats and how traders buy in grams, but prices on the international markets are in dollars. Show them how and where on the internet they can get the price of gold in grams in your currency, minute by minute.

Explain in detail the significance of karats and that they represent the percentage of pure gold in a given item. Teach them the marks for the diferent karats, 375 for 9ct for example. Make them learn them and test them.

Explain about the value being based on the weight per karat. Usualy you will tell them what your prices are that day. But sometimes if there are sudden movements that are significant the price might change. If a customer came in at 10am but prices dropped by $50 by 2pm would you still honour the 10am price? You need to establish a policy. Personally I would honour the first priceand give up any profit if necessary. Not only is it the fair thing to do but it is interesting that if you pay fair prices and treat people with respect and courtesy how quickly you will get business by recommendation. This is of course the best way of all!

I have read that some gold traders buy gold from dentists, but when I tried this I was told that actually they buy more gold than they sell. Perhaps in depends on the country and locality in which you live.

Networking also helps a lot with this business so don't be embarrassed about telling people what you do and giving them a card. Teach your staff to do the same and perhaps pay a small commission on introductions or even on deals that the shop has done.

Another thing is the way the staff treat customers. Surly, miserable looking people seam to be in lots of shops now. Teach your people the three first steps.' GREET. SMILE. THANK. A smile costs nothing and relaxes the customer, a 'Good Morning' encourages conversation and a 'Thank You' when you give the customer his money encourages him to like you and not only perhaps come back, but also to recommend your shop to others.

Teaching staff to weigh jewelry is obviously simple. However, when there is a valuable stone involved such as a good sized diamond I would suggest that a second opinion is obtained. Most people will leave an item for an hour or two or for as long as it will take you to arrive. If you are not at that point experienced enough to make an offer take it to your friendly jeweler.

If the stones in a ring are not diamonds or known to be genuine rubies or emeralds teach your staff to just base their price on the total weight value. Accept the fact that sometimes you wil lmiss a good deal, but at all costs don't take the risk of a bad deal.

With a new member of staff let them test and weigh their own jewelry and also some of your stock. Everyone is nervous at first, so be relaxed and congratulate them if they carry out the process correctly. If they make a mistake don't criticize, just explain again. Let them engage in role play with both you and they being customers and buyers. Do lots of this.

So we have covered gold valuing, weighing etc. The same principle applies to platinum or white gold, the value of white gold is usually the same as 18ct.

Silver is tested in the same way as gold except that you need the correct acid. Value is of course much lower than gold and so only solid silver is worth buying unless you become an expert on some of the famous silver plate makers. Get a book from the library, English and Scottish silver is particularly interesting and silver marks will show the town where the item was made and it's age. It is a very interesting subject.

Silver values are strange in that they can move about quite a lot. What is interesting about silver is that at this moment in time the world production of silver is only about 40% of what is consumed in medical equipment, computers etc. The diference is coming from melting down existing silver items. As an investment silver could be a very interesting proposition. The disadvantage when compared with gold is that it takes up more space in relation to the value and can tarnish.

Silver can be bought from the general public but if you can remove it easily it can also be found in old X ray machines and other items. Silver coins are only worth buying if they are solid silver. If the magnet picks them up then they are not solid. Pay 75% of the spot price because most silver coins will be worth more as collectors pieces than the value of the silver.

Other coins do have value, especially kruger rands and guineas. The value will be more than the gold value. Look on the internet for coin values and offer 50% of 'retail' prices.

WHERE TO SELL

So far we have dealt with selling to refiners who will melt down your gold or silver items and usualy pay you 95% of the spot gold bullion price. However most will only buy 100 grams or upwards and in the early days it may take you a few weeks to reach that level. Others will take smaller quantities, but will charge you a smelting fee. Therefore you may have to deal with a middleman in the beginning. These chaps will buy from other small dealers and because their volume can be very high the refiners will even pay them more than usual. Most are honest, although there was one in our area who recently killed himself because he had misappropriated the funds. To avoid this you must first find a known honest buyer. He will probanly call on you when you open your shop but if you ask around pawn brokers etc one of them will probably be a buyer. Before you go ahead check that they will pay you immediate cash. Also weigh everything yourself and list it and show him the list because he may go into his little back room to do the weighing and calculating. If he knows that you are serious, organized and business like he will be less likely to try and cheat you.

Apart from selling your purchases to refiners and gold dealers you can also sell any quality items to jewelers. If you have stuff which is in good condition and especialy if it has stones you may well get a better price from a jeweler than a dealer. This will not usually apply to cheap low value items but the better quality pieces, especially 18ct. This will involve lots of legwork, but you could build up a good conection.

STONES AND DIAMONDS

DIAMONDS. What a fascinating subject. The endless variations of colour and brilliance. The sheer thrill of looking at something beautiful.

Although diamonds are the most valuable stones and do have a certain magic and fascination there are many other beautiful stones with wonderful colours.

As a Gold Trader you will be offered diamonds for sale and although there follows some indications of how to value you really are advised to seek a qualified second opinion as values depend on so many factors. Also, do beware of uncut diamonds that are offered as there are a great many illegal diamonds around. In fact I was once selling a farm that I owned in Africa and a bag of wonderful diamonds was emptied on my coffee table as an offer for the farm. The property was for sale for six million rand and the uncut value of the diamonds was fourteen million. How they glistened as they cascaded onto the table, the light reflected from the many diferent shades. There was a certain magic in the moment and how tempting it was! Thankfully sanity intervened and I declined. The characters involved were arrested some months later together with the farmer involved.

Most people think that the size of a diamond mainly determines its value. Although a big diamond with all the other qualities is worth much more than a small one, the other factors are highly relevant. There are four 'Cs' that you must learn about before you even begin to understand the possibilities of value. They are colour, clarity, cut and carrat. You may have noticed that the word carrat has been spelt elsewhere as karat, either spelling can be used.

Most of the diamonds that you will be offered will be small diamond chips in rings. They have very little value, but if you take them out of the rings that you have bought they will add up to a tidy sum over time. If however they are larger diamonds of good clarity, appealing colour ,fashionable cut and good size the value can be very considerable. At the time of writing [2012] the following are approximate prices'

1 ct circa $2000.   2ct circa $5000-$6000.   3ct $15000 -$25000. However, I strongly urge you to take professional advice before making an offer. With the help of Skype you will be able to get an idea of value quite quickly and you might intimate a price to the customer subject to a second opinion. Never be tempted by greed to part with large sums of money until you are certain of both value and provenance. Of course you will have carefully used your diamond tester at the very beginning to be sure that the stone is indeed a diamond and not one of the incredibly good man made fakes!

In their natural uncut and unpolished state diamonds are not at all attractive and look like glassy pebbles. The range of colours is quite large and although clear diamonds that look like sparkling glass are what most of us first expect in a diamond there are in fact a range of colours. The most admired is probably the clear blue, but there are blacks, yellows and many other 'fancy' diamonds.

When assessing a diamond look first for flaws. If the stone is absolutely clear then that is a good beginning. Look for spots and slight marks that mar the perfection of the stone. Obviously the weight is highly relevant and if you were buying a legal uncut diamond expect to lose about 50%of the weight with cutting. But until you become an expert get an opinion from your qualified contact. Incidentally, you will have little difficulty in finding dealers to help you as they will make a good profit if they buy and sell on.

The way that a diamond is cut is very relevant to the value. Like most things fashions change. At the time of writing [2012] the most popular diamond cuts are round, square and emerald. Heart shaped or pillow shaped are less in demand.

EMERALDS are the second most valuable stone. They have a special greenness about them that makes them so beautiful and appealing. The green does vary and the one considered the most beautiful is the colour of fresh green grass and will be intense and clear. Emeralds can also be pale leaf green or the colour of green fir. One interesting historical fact is that Caesar collected emeralds because of his belief in their healing power. As they have taken millions of years to be formed there is certainly something special about this stone. There is no easy way to recognize a genuine emerald. It takes experience to know. However, bear in mind that the value of stones in jewelry so often relates to the quality of the gold. It would be very unusual to find an emerald in a 9ct ring.

RUBIES are the third most valuable stone and as red is the most popular of colours, the colour alone gives the ruby a certain appeal, but value will depend and the vividness and sparkle The name comes from the Latin word 'ruber'. Red is the predominant colour of this 'July' stone, but there are many variations ranging from pink to daekest purple. The most precious are those with the colour called 'pigeon blood.', Mostly used in 18ct gold jewelery

Apart from the main three stones there are scores of other stones of immense beauty. Many are not particularly valuable but from a Gold Trader's point of view all are worth saving. Occassionaly something special might occur.

TOPAZ is a beautiful stone in shades of yellow,brown,pink, light blue and wine red.Often regarded as the 'Sun Stone.'

SAPHIRES was known as the 'The Stone of Heaven'. Although the dominant colour is blue variations are cornflower blue,royal blue,cobalt blue, marine blue,ice blue, electric blue and many others.

CHRYOBERYL is very fascinating stone in a range of greens and yellows. There are three varieties 'Cat's eye, chrysoberyl. What is so appealing about these stones is the way that they reflect light.

MOONSTONE A shimmering stone, found mainly in Ceylon. Colours range from shimmering silvery white soft gray,blue.green or orange. It is the stone of those born in June.

OPAL is found in many colours-orange,green, blue cream and white. It is not usualy one complete colour but ha shades or spots of other colours and tones.

PERIDOT. A shining green mostly transluscent stone

JADE. . Also known as 'The Jewel Of Heaven.' Beautiful stone used largely for carving both pendants and small statues. Colours are green,orange,mauve,yellow,white and many other variations. Being arelatively hard stone Jade was used during the Stone Age in tools and only became of predominantly ornamental use much later.

LAPIS LAZULI. Is a rock and not a mineral combination like other stones. It is mainly dark blue and some rocks have fascinating and desirable pattern formations caused by tiny flecks of pyrite crystals which glitter like metallic gold..

MALACHITE. This is a beautifully patterned glossy green stone and one of the rarest of ornamental stones.

TURQUOISE. Much admired by the Pharaos this fascinating stone is found in both green and blue. It was mainly used as part of very valuable pieces, but is now much more widely used.

MARKETING

The statistics for business start ups are not encouraging. Figures vary from country to country, but the average seems to be that three out of ten businesses fail within twelve months and the others steadily one by one after that until only one will be left in ten years. Although this may sound disappointing there do seem to be a number of things that the failures have in common and certain specific policies that lead to success. Often great success!

Quite apart from the wonderful feeling that comes when you hand over your successful business to your kids or put it under professional management and go on a long cruise, it is also good to realize that small businesses are the backbone of many economies in the world. When policies of supporting small businesses are created by government nemployment almost always falls rapidly. This doesn't even mean that governments must support small businesses in the beginning wth grants or other cash incentives. Just cutting out red tape and encouraging the banks to take a little more risk is often enough to create an economy sympathetic to small business. Also, everyone should bear in mind that every big business started out as a small one.

Capital is often the main cause of failure. In my own personal experience this is not necessarily a shortage of money to start the business, it's more the question of what do you and the family live on whilst you are building it up? Most businesses take three years before they show substantial net profits, so think about the cost of living problem. If you have an enthusiastic partner, indulgent parent, part time evening job or a pension you will do it and have a good solid proft making business, or even a very big business if you want to that far.

If you keep a watchful eye on your expenditure you should break even quite quickly and be making a monthly profit within six months.Apart from capital to start a business you need to think carefully about your costs and you must make a business plan. If you are seeking bank finance you will certainly need to do this and also a cash flow forecast. There are lots of retired bookeepers around who will be running small part time businesses. Discuss your plans with one and ask for a price to prepare a good presentation for you in a professional way.

As this is a low cost business there are not many serious expenses. Rental will probably be your biggest and this will obviously vary from area to area. However a small unit in a busy area will not necessarily be that expensive. Visibility is an important factor in this business and if your shop is hidden away in an alley you will only get business if you advertise in newsapers etc or if you are allowed to put a billboard on the pavement. Goving out leaflets to passers by would also roduce a little business, but not much. So go for the most visible premises that you can afford and spend less on advertising.

Your projected expenses per month might look like this;

Rent $3000 Advertising $2000. Tel $200. Miscellaneous $1000. Total $6200.Per month.

Month one you buy 10 rings weighing 5 grams each. You pay $600 each and sell for $1000. Gross profit $4000. Loss $2200

Month two you buy 20 rings for 5 grams each [total $12000] you sell for $1000 each. Gross profit $8000. Net profit $1800.

Month by month your turnover should grow as you become better known and you start doing pawn and selling on the better jewelery, within one year you should be trading very profitably.

You will initialy have to do some advertising in the local paper. These should be in blocks if you can afford them, but if you are in some big city like London or New York where advertising is very expensive [although the circulation may also be enormous] you may have to just run lineage adds. An example of a lineage add would be 'GOLD WANTED. TRY OTHERS BUYERS AND THEN CALL ME. LOW OVERHEADS MEAN THE BEST PRICES. MR GOLD…….

An example of a block ad that works, especially if you take it as a 'reverse block' which means white on black MIGHT BE AS FOLLOWS;

CASH FOR GOLD

GOLD WANTED   EARING WANTED

BEST PRICES

ANY CONDITION

AND ANY OTHER

GOLD, JEWELERY, SILVER

BEST, BEST PRICES   ODD ITEMS FOR CASH

EVEN BROKEN OR OLD

JEWELRY, SILVER, DIAMONDS   JEWELERY, GOLD WATCHES

ITEMS. DIAMONDS ETC

MR GOLD TEL....   EVEN BROKEN. SILVER, DIAMONDS

MR GOLD TEL

999 GOLD ST

There are many other ideas and you must watch the successful competition. What are they doing that's so right!

When you start your gold business you must read and memorize the important points in this short guide. You must look and sound as if you know what you are doing. You must be Miss or Mister Sucessful. Apart from sounding knowledgeable think about the shops that you like to do business with. Apart from good produce and fair prices they also 'Greet'; 'Smile'; and 'Thank'.

You must be a peoples person and if that doesn't come easy to you don't worry, it will if you try. I promise!

Apart from your business plan you must have a vision of what you want to achieve. If you want one good very profitable shop visualize it and put a vision board on your wall and pin a picture of a smart and attractive jewelers. Also, what car do you dream of? Pin a picture of one on your vision board. If you are looking for the right partner pin a picture taken from a newspaper of the type. In my experience vision is everything and you must look at your vision board every day and NEVER DOUBT THAT YOU CAN ACHIEVE ANYTHING.

Every day visualize all your desires and see it all like a movie actually happening and it will.

GOLDEN RULE EIGHT: IF YOU VISUALISE, YOUR DREAMS WILL COME TRUE.

PROFITABILITY

One of the most successful business people in the world has a policy of dealing with all complaints personally. He sells exhausts and if there is a complaint about the work he puts it right personally. Apart from good products at good prices, he uses the personal touch and almost everyone recommends his company. He started out as a mechanic and his company is now international. There is no doubt that the personal approach is one of the biggest steps to success.

You must aim for the same kind of business contact. Apart from all the obvious things about being charming and friendly you must also be fair. If you are you will pay more for some of your gold or jewelery items than unscrupulous dealers but you will also be doing the right thing. The interesting fact about this is that in the long run honest and fair Gold Traders do the best. This is because the best advertising of all is recommendation. In my early days I made a few mistakes and paid solid gold prices for a few items that were actually plate. At the time I was really sick inside about my mistake, but as time went on I learned that the lucky sellers had recommended me over and over again. I am not sure if I got all my money back from the extra trade but I would like to think so.

Knowledge is power. You have taken the first step and even if you have only read the guide once, by now you will already know many things about the gold business that you didn't know before. However the learning process goes on forever. There is a plethora of information about gold and jewelery, never stop reading and if you can take part time courses on jewelery making etc. One chap that I know drives around Nice in the south of France in his Rolls Royce. He started out by taking an evening course about making jewelery. Then he acquired more knowledge and bought a diamond necklace at an auction. Not only could he tell that it was a real diamond necklace, but it was sold with the karat size and quality, so he knew what he was buying. He broke the necklace up and bought some extra gold chains and turned the one necklace into six which he sold. He multiplied his money ten times and has never looked back. Apart from knowing what he is doing he cultivates a lot of people and sells to his neywork. People buy because he is cheaper than a retail jeweler. So start networking!

Apart from buying gold, silver and diamonds you can more than double your business by lending money against items. Do it fairly as I have suggested earlier in the guide and people will recommend you and your fabulous income from buying and selling gold will probably double. Open a nice little jewelery shop and sell the best items that you have bought and you will have created a third income stream.If you do it all correctly you really will become a millionaire.

If you are very ambitious and brave think about buying gold on a national scale by post. Your advertising cost will be huge, but your premises costs will be lower. The biggest challenge is staff, but if you can solve this problem and treat your people well you could really hit the big time.

However, if you want the good life but don't want the responsibility of a chain of shops or a huge national operation just keep it simple and follow the rules in this guide, depending on how hard you work you will either make a comfortable income or a lot of money.

Good luck!

Mr. Gold

www.ingramcontent.com/pod-product-compliance
Lightning Source LLC
Chambersburg PA
CBHW070725180526
45167CB00004B/1622